Hameed's House

Mini Mu'min Du'a Series #7

www.Mini-Mumin.com

Copyright © 2013 Mini Mu'min Publications

All rights reserved. This publication may not be reproduced in whole or in part by any means whatsoever without written permission from the copyright owner.

Introduction

All praise is due to Allah the Most High, may Allah send His blessings on the Prophet Muhammad (saw), his family, his companions, and those who follow him in righteousness until the Day of Judgment.

"And remember your Lord by your tongue and within yourself, humbly and in awe, without loudness, by words in the morning and the afternoon, and be not among those who are neglectful." (Holy Qur'an 7:205)

The **Mini Mu'min Du'a Series** is designed to help you teach your child essential Islamic supplications and the situations in which they would be used. Each book focuses on a single topic, with key vocabulary highlighted. These key words can then serve as a tool to remind your child of important points. All supplications are shown in Arabic text, translation, and transliteration. For any assertions regarding fiqh we have provided textual proofs, from the Qur'an and authentic Sunnah of the Prophet (saw), at the bottom of the relevant page. Each story is accompanied by original artwork, but in accordance with Islamic beliefs we do not use human or animal images.

Transliteration has been provided here as a means to help those who do not know Arabic to teach supplications to their children; but it must be noted that all transliteration is imperfect and cannot accurately represent Arabic sounds in their entirety. We therefore encourage anyone who uses our books to use the transliteration as a tool, but not an end in itself, and to eventually learn the supplications in the original Arabic.

In some cases, sounds will be represented in the transliteration (because they are present in the Arabic text) that will not actually be pronounced. These generally occur at the end of a supplication and are related to the Arabic rules for pausing and stopping. To clarify this for non-Arabic speakers, we have placed brackets [ ] around those sounds in the transliteration that would not be pronounced when reciting the supplication.

Thank you for purchasing this book, may Allah benefit both you and your child through it, forgive us for any errors we have made, and benefit us in this life and the Hereafter if there is any good in it.

When snowflakes gently fall,
And icicles sparkle bright,

Hameed loves to ride his sled,
Down hills all fluffy and white...

But when it gets too **cold** to play,
And his cheeks glow red and rosy-

Hameed always goes back **home**,
Where it is **snug** and **cozy**!

When flowers start to bloom,
And the grass begins to grow,

Hameed plays out in the garden,
Planting seeds in a neat little row...

But when clouds gather overhead,
Bringing a sudden spring **rainstorm**-

Hameed always goes back **home**,
Where it is **dry** and **warm**!

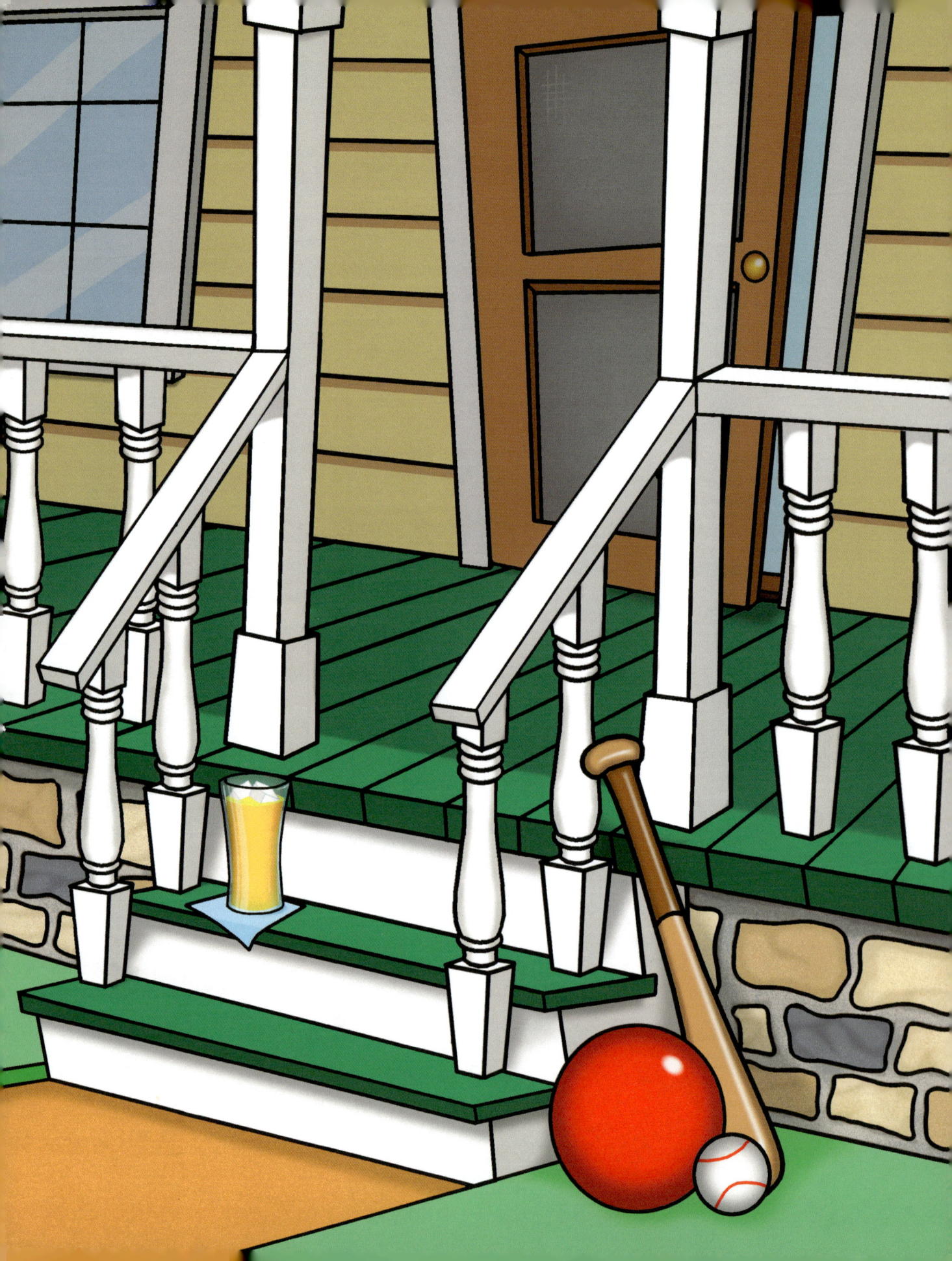

When the days are long and hot,
Hameed is outside building forts,

Or running around with his friends,
Playing all kinds of summer sports…

But when the **sun burns** brightly,
And he needs some lemonade-

Hameed always goes back **home**,
Where he can **cool off** in the **shade**!

When autumn leaves are falling,
Hameed likes to pile them high,

Then he jumps right in the middle-
And watches the colors fly!...

But when the **wind** grows **chilly**,
And it's time to go to bed-

Hameed always goes back **home**,
Where he can **rest** his sleepy head!

Home is where you find your **family**,
And bring your **friends** to play,

It's the place where you always go,
At the end of a long and busy day.

Home is a place that is **safe**,
A place of **peacefulness** and **rest**,

Where you feel like a baby bird,
Snuggled down in a comfy nest.

Homes can be very different-
Made of glass, metal, and bricks;

Or a simple hut made of mud,
With a roof of grass and sticks.

Homes come in all shapes and sizes,
But one thing is always the same-

When a Muslim **leaves** their **home**,
They always make ***du'a*** in Allah's name.[1]

---

[1] Narrated Anas ibn Malik (ra): the Prophet (saw) said, "When a man goes out of his house and says: '*In the name of Allah, I have placed my trust in Allah, there is no might and no power except by Allah.*' the following will be said to him at that time: 'You are guided, defended, and protected.' The devils will go far from him and another devil will say, 'How can you deal with a man who has been guided, defended, and protected?' " (Abu Dawud 41/5076, See also Al-Albaani's *Sahih Kalimat-Tayyib* #44)

Du'a Made When Leaving the House (Part 1)

بِسْمِ اللَّهِ، تَوَكَّلْتُ عَلَى اللَّهِ،
وَ لَا حَوْلَ وَ لَا قُوَّةَ إِلَّا بِاللَّهِ

"Bismillaah[i], tawakkaltu 'alallah[i], wa laa hawla wa laa quwwata illa billah."

(In the name of Allah, I have placed my trust in Allah, there is no might and no power except by Allah.[2])

---

[2] Abu Dawud 4/325, At-Tirmidthi 5/490. See also Al-Albaani, *Sahih At-Tirmidthi 3/151.*

But once you are out of your home,
You could get **lost** along your way,

Or make a **mistake** or **harm** someone,
And end up having a very bad day!

So, we don't just walk out the door,
Wave to our family and say-
"Good-bye!"

Instead, we stop and make **du'a**[3] again,
While **looking up**[4] at the beautiful sky…

---

[3] Supplication Made When Leaving the House (Part 2) - Abu Dawud, Ibn Maajah, Nasaai, At-Tirmidthi. See also Al-Albaani, *Sahih At-Tirmidthi* 3/152 and *Sahih Ibn Maajah* 2/336.

[4] Narrated Umm Salamah, Ummul Mu'mineen (raa): The Apostle of Allah (saw) never went out of my house without raising his eyes to the sky and saying, "*O Allah! I seek refuge in You lest I misguide others, or I am misguided by others, lest I cause others to err or I am caused to err, lest I abuse others or be abused, and lest I behave foolishly or meet with the foolishness of others.*" (Abu Dawud 41/5075, See also Al-Albaani's *Sahih Kalimat-Tayyib* #45)

Du'a Made When Leaving the House (Part 2)

اللَّهُمَّ إِنِّي أَعُوذُ بِكَ أَنْ أَضِلَّ، أَوْ أُضَلَّ، أَوْ أَزِلَّ، أَوْ أُزَلَّ، أَوْ أَظْلِمَ، أَوْ أُظْلَمَ، أَوْ أَجْهَلَ، أَوْ يُجْهَلَ عَلَيَّ

"Allaahumma innee a'oothu bika 'an adhilla, aw udhall[a], aw azilla, aw uzall[a], aw adhlima, aw udhlam[a], aw ajhala, aw yujhala 'alayy[a]."

(Oh Allah, I seek refuge in You lest I misguide others, or I am misguided by others, lest I cause others to err or I am caused to err, lest I abuse others or be abused, and lest I behave foolishly or meet with the foolishness of others.)

Now you will be **guided**[5]
And **defended** as you go about,

Because you remembered,
To make du'a when you went out!

So, whether you go out to play,
Or to learn your ABC's and math-

You will be **protected**
As you go along your path!

---
[5] See footnote #1

No matter where you live-
In a big city with noise and lights,

Or far away in a quiet desert,
With shifting sands and starry nights…

When it's time to **go back home**,
After you finish your busy day,

Make sure to **remember Allah** again,
To keep the **uninvited guest** away…

You see, when you go **home**,
Shaytaan wants to come with you,

So he can have a place to **rest**,
And get some **dinner**, too!

But Shaytaan is not your friend,
You don't want him in your house-

He's a **pest** you **keep out**-
Like a bug or a munching mouse!

No need for extra locks or fences,
No need to yell or shout,

Just remember **Allah**[6] when you **enter**-
It's that **EASY** to keep **Shaytaan out**!

Then get **blessings** for yourself,
And the people in your home too,

When you give **greetings** to them,
And they give greetings back to you!

---

[6] Jabir bin 'Abdullah (ra) reported: Allah's Messenger (saw) as saying, "When a person enters his house and mentions the name of Allah at the time of entering it and while eating food, Satan says (addressing himself) 'You have no place to spend the night and no evening meal', but when he enters without mentioning the name of Allah, Satan says, 'You have found a place to spend the night', and when he does not mention the name of Allah while eating food, he (Satan) says, 'You have found a place to spend the night and an evening meal.' " (Muslim 23/5006, See also Al-Albaani's *Sahih Kalimat-Tayyib* #46)

Islamic Greeting

السَّلَامُ عَلَيْكُمْ

"As-salaamu 'alaikum"

(Peace be upon you![7])

Reply to Islamic Greeting

وَ عَلَيْكُمُ السَّلَامْ

"Wa 'alaikumus-salaam"

(And upon you be peace!)

---

[7] Narrated Anas (ra): The Messenger of Allah (saw) said to me: "O my son, when you enter upon your family, give greetings- it shall be a blessing on you and on the family of your house." (At-Tirmidthi, See also Al-Albaani's *Sahih Kalimat-Tayyib* #47)

So, when Hameed goes back home,
He does just what we've been told-

He **remembers Allah** as he enters,
Leaving Shaytaan outside in the cold!

Then he **greets** his family warmly,
And they sit down together to eat,

Alhamdu lillaah[8]-
Safe and sound in his **home**,
Hameed's **happiness** is complete!

---

[8] Arabic phrase meaning "Praise is for Allah"

Remember Allah when you go outside,
And when you come home again, too-

So **Shaytaan** will stay **out** of your house;
And **Allah** will **guide** and **protect** you!

Home is where you live and play,
Where you sleep and dream your dreams,

But now you know, that for a Muslim,
A **home** is **so much more** than it seems!

Other available titles in the Mini Mu'min Du'a Series:

Batool's Bedtime Story
Bilal's Bakery
Fatimah's First Fasting Day
Jameelah Gets Dressed
Muhammed Goes to the Masjid
Saliha Sneezes
Waheeda the Wudoo' Wonder
Waleed Wakes Up

and many more!...

Visit our online bookstore at:

www.Mini-Mumin.com

Made in the USA
Charleston, SC
13 January 2014